THE NIGHT BEFORE JESUS

Herbert Brokering

Concordia Publishing House
St. Louis

Copyright © 1977 Concordia Publishing House,
3558 South Jefferson Avenue, St. Louis, MO 63118
Manufactured in the United States of America

5 6 7 8 9 10 11 12 13 14   98 97 96 95 94 93 92 91 90 89

'Twas the night before Jesus when all through the earth,

every creature was stirring for a new Baby's birth.

The people were looking straight up and then down,

to the left and the right, both in country and town.

Some faces were watching far out in the sky
believing God's Son would be soon coming by.
In Bethlehem children were snug in their beds,
with dreams of olives and figs in their heads.

Sheep had just baaed their last sleepy bleat,

and the shepherds were tired, weary and beat,

When up in the air there arose such a clatter,

The shepherds saw angels and asked, "What's

the matter?"

They jumped to their feet and stood straight and tall

and saw thousands of angels, and heard angels call.

It sounded like glory, looked bright as can be;

it was hard to believe, it was so hard to see.

When what to their wondering eyes did appear

but glory around them, so loud and so near.

It happened so sudden, it happened so quick.

Was it real? Was it true? Or was it a trick?

More rapid than eagles the shepherds then came,

found Mary and Joseph, and whispered His name.

"It is Jesus, Jehovah, Messiah, the Son,

Emmanuel, the Lord. He is all and each one."

They fell to their knees way down on the ground;

how good to receive Him, the One they had found.

The shepherds saw Jesus; they almost did cry,

for Jesus their Savior had surely come by.

So straight up the hillside their running feet flew,

with their eyes full of Jesus, their hearts now like new.

Far away, Wise Men stood on some roof,

searching the skies for Biblical proof.

Night after night they hunted with care

for a sign of God's love in some stars up there.

"There!" each one shouted. "Out in the east!"

And they mounted with haste their two-humped beasts.

One Wise Man with gold had a little round tummy.

The frankincense Wise Man smelled yummy yum yummy.

The gift of rare myrrh had been packed in a can

for Jesus would need it when He was a man.

They were soon filled with questions from head

down to toe.

They asked, "Where's the new King; we truly

must know?"

They traveled so long and traveled so far,

and followed their hearts and came to the star.

Each face of the Wise Men was grim for a while,

then slowly each cheek returned to a smile,

They saw that God gave His Son to the earth,

They took up God's Gift, putting theirs on the earth.

There was no more to do; there was no more to say.

This was God's world, and this was God's day.

As the Baby blinked slowly while turning His head;

The Wise Men knew then they had nothing to dread.

They spoke not a word as they headed for home;

they were thankful to God that Christ Jesus had come.

Christ was on earth, and old was like new.

Now people could see what God could do.

When children hurt and old men whistle,

where there are fir trees and dry prickly thistle,

it's the night before Jesus, from ground to the sky,

and Jesus, the Brother, will surely come by.

So we know and you know that God is in sight.

Good morning to all, and to all a good night.